Megan Beech was the winner of the Poetry Society's SLAMbassadors national youth slam 2011, and the Poetry Rivals UK under 18 slam 2011. She has performed at the Southbank Centre, Glastonbury, Latitude and Larmer Tree Festivals as well as for institutions including The British Museum, Keats House, UCL and the University of Cambridge. She recorded her poetry with actress Fiona Shaw CBE for the cultural Olympiad project, 'Peace Camp' and is currently an undergraduate in English at King's College London.

# Megan Beech

# When I Grow Up I Want to be MARY BEARD

Burning Eye

This edition published by Burning Eye Books 2013

Burning Eye Books
15 West Hill, Portishead, BS20 6LG

www.burningeye.co.uk

@burningeye

ISBN 978 1 90913 626 7

'Megan Beech is full to the brim with everything a powerful woman needs to take over the world: passion, heart, humour and an uncanny knack for making words bend to her every whim.'
Vanessa Kisuule

'Meg Beech is a dynamo of the spoken word scene. As comfortable invoking The Tempest as Kate Tempest, she playfully draws on a bookish love of literature and a live engagement with the world around her to produce lines that rattle across the page like hailstones.'
Ally Davies
former Education Coordinator at The Poetry Society

'Megan Beech coaxes shy words out of their shells and makes them party on the page; suddenly they all connect to each other in ways that even they weren't expecting. She is a master of intricate yet punchy rhyme and rhythm, and a young poet with the potential to light up the scene for years to come.'
Simon Mole

# CONTENTS

# When I Grow Up I Want to be Mary Beard

When I grow up I want to be Mary Beard.
A classy, classic, classicist,
intellectually revered.
Wickedly wonderful and wise
full to brim with life,
while explaining the way in which Caligula died,
on BBC prime time.
And I would like, like her, to shine.
The kind inclined to speak her mind,
refined and blinding.
Yet I am finding
it tough
to grow up
in a world where Twitter is littered
with abuse towards women,
where intelligent, eminent, eloquent
females are met with derision.
Because she should be able to analyse Augustus' dictums
or early AD epithets,
without having to scroll through death, bomb and rape threats.
Do not tell me this is just the internet
or a public figure deserves everything they get.
Because this isn't just about one academic, it's endemic
in this society enmeshed in sexist rhetoric.
I cannot live accepting it!
Because when I grow up I want to be Mary Beard,
to wear shiny converse and converse on conquerors
and pioneers.
A sheer delight, an igniter of young minds,
but never a victim.
Like Minerva herself, a goddess of wisdom.

# There is Poetry

'Poetry is stupid!'
'Poetry's for losers!'
Well that might be the view that you pursue and that's cool,
but I believe that poetry's for choosers, for dictionary abusers,
from pensioners to preschoolers.
It's for people who are unashamed to take to a stage
and convey their words in a way that states,
'I mean what I say'.
Because I believe in the power of the spoken word,
that saying a verse that gets heard
gives me some worth on this Earth.
I'm just surfing this wordplay wave from pen to page
and believe me it can take you to the strangest of places.
It's been a couple years since it became clear
I might have something to say,
then suddenly I found myself shouting down a microphone
on a Glastonbury Festival stage.
All the same, I used to feel afraid too,
because when you put yourself out there
people tend to criticise you,
and that's cruel, not cool
and it shouldn't affect what you choose to do.
So if like me you've got this verbal fur ball
hanging in the back of your throat,
then come up here and give it a go.
Let what you've got show.
Let your greatness glow.
Let your confidence grow like Jack's beanstalk.
Talk the talk.
Deliver like the stalk.
Fly like an eagle and soar, throw lightning bolts like Thor.

Use the force like you're in Star Wars,
charge like a lion that roars,
pop like a champagne cork and bask in your applause.
That is what it's for.
Because when I stand here speaking in stanza
I feel like I hold the whole world in my hands.
I slam and therefore I am.
So never be afraid for yourself to express
because it's what keeps people going,
through the dark and the madness.
And yes I choose to leave the politricking to the politicians,
the mind boggling puzzles to the mathematicians.
I just scribble down poems like it's my life long mission,
don't really care what people say
I sit create and chase my vision.
So be bold, be brave and make that decision:
to bare your heart
and make a mark on the world that we live in.
'Cause only you can choose
not to let your mind be imprisoned,
so who cares what people say?
Just sit create and chase your visions.

# Ansisters

Minute-old miniature goddess,
bloom of womb flowering promise.
Not yet conscious of concepts that condition from conception,
feminine self-dissection,
where acceptance is dependent on
deceptive, projected perfection.
There is no protection from the societal lesson
that to thrive is to strive for style over substance,
to take pride in depriving your mind of sustenance.
Mental malnourishment fed by media encouragement.
She seeks flourishing
but she will spend life struggling
in debris of sanctified sexuality.
Stripped of grace and modesty,
a body bound commodity,
poster girl, pin-up misogyny.
But she is possibility's progeny, a self-fulfilling prophecy,
more capable than she is able to conceive
in a world where undressed, repressed, bare breast
are expressed as the holy trinity of femininity,
so pervasively preached, she cannot help but listen,
until she's restricted to the fiction that her body is a prison.
It isn't.
It's a prism.
A vision of light,
a spectrum, exceptionally constructed to shine.
Future divine,
fewer more primed to change the world in a whisper,
to voice the void with our Ansisters.

And History is typically written by victors,
but she is kissed by lips of scripture,
words of women, driven unflinching resistors,
who've had to fight to define their existence.
But she could rewrite the script in an instant,
though infant,
she is infinite, intricate author of women,
daughter of wisdom.
Tongue never caught in the rhythm of victim.
She is future's incumbent.
She is styled out of substance.

# Toleranter

Who am I?
A person who resides in a place
that appears to have been
painted by a passionless Picasso
on a particularly unproductive day
in a palette of pallid purples and pavement greys.
And every day it feels the same,
leaving me shaken, inspiration not stirred.
But I've learnt:
it's not about the place,
it's the state of the space between
your head and your heartbeat,
about finding a cause and not feeling floored by the ground
beneath your feet.
And sometimes this world gets so
maddening and saddening and bleak
but I still believe.
I'll hit the street armed with a Geobar and an open heart
that stop starts sharp when I see the people
content to let the future fall apart.
I'll stand up and play my part but I won't wear a mask.
It's society's face but I'm baring its scars.
Not looking to leaders, just a jump lead and a speeding car,
so far and fast from here I can depart.
But I still cling with all my heart,
to the kind of kindness that kindles the coldest of camp-fires,
and lean to the lyrics of lefty songs
written to right the wrongs
that don't belong in a world
we claim to be
so modern and so strong.

Because I am the poet who won't stand stoic
and watch the chaos ensue,
and I see the devastation in this nation
tangled up in Cameron's blue.
And I'm no longer tolerant so I'm toleranting
because I'm angry and I don't know what else to do.
But I refuse to feel bruised by the state of the news
and choose to pursue the view
that one day hope will rise as high as the soaring price of fuel.
I renew my faith in words and verse
and saying what you dare,
in plucking on guitar strings and expressing something rare.
Because the message that I blare is where my soul lies bare.
And the Politrickers and city slickers
probably don't care who I am.
But at least I am someone who cares
and who's prepared to give a damn.

# Lon(e)don

'Evening Standard' on standard London evenings,
this city is heaving.
Chests beating,
palpitate with the weight of their innermost demons.
But every face remains unfeeling.
And population statistics appear to deceive.
Because in a city of eight million,
I'm alone as a civilian
and my days, I am filling
with theatre seats for one and vermilion Waterloo sunsets
And 'I am in paradise', lost
in a fog of anonymity
and that's part of the reason why I love this city.
My liturgies are these littered streets,
this constant hum the song on my hymnal sheet.
But today I am struggling to find belief.
All is pinstripes and traffic lights and Boris bikes and concrete.
I let it conquer me and anyone can see
this place doesn't belong to me.
Because I still have to wait for the man to turn green
before I cross the street
and the need to rush to get crushed in tube doors is lost on me.
All I'm after is kindness not diamond encrusted dreams,
because we knot ourselves in ties and then claim to be free.
But my soul too is shackled,
to the leaves and bark of Richmond Park's tallest tree,
and the shadow of St Paul's as the sun falls in evening breeze.
Those like me prepared to shiver to watch Shakespeare
outdoors for free,
the blue plaques that track the literary history of every street.
The Big Issue seller on Fleet Street that I pass every day,

who offers a pleasant smile despite me never having change.
To the change and the range and the depth of human kind
who populate this city and flourish side by side.
The sense of feeling you're alive,
that vitality survives behind the garish glare of neon signs.
My London: brutal, beautiful and wild
must have some others who see the world through my eyes.
But until I find some and I settle in this city as my home,
it is a comfort to know
that when in Lon(e)don you are never alone.

# Binding (for Ally)

I ran into you.
Foyles Bookstore, Southbank, Bank Holiday Monday.
Between the Dickens and the Dostoyevsky.
Between the mid-afternoon sun's slow sleepwalk
into early evening.
Between the numbness and returning of feeling.
Serendipitous surprise breeds symbiotic smiles,
and for the first time in a while mine is not furtively failing
or book-ended by medication.
Yet I have left a trail of tears,
a tempestuous Thames trickling down London lanes
and lines down face like blotted pages.
On your shoulder.
On Covent Garden concrete.
On Bakerloo Line platforms heading for opposite destinations,
through after-parties in Southbank Centre basements.
In conversations by industrial metal bins,
King's Way,
bus wait shivering.
Frightened, fragile and failing.
You spoke me forward, wrote my foreword with four words.
'You're not OK Meg' and with that said I tried my best to mend.
With folks like you to bind me better,
you found me
in the fiction section of Foyles,
pages slowly sticking back together.

# Snogging on the Circle Line

Sitting and trying not to stare on the train
at the chain of saliva, vein-like and pale,
with as many twists and turns as this underground rail.

Snogging on the circle line,
they should implement a fine.
I mean I'm fine with public affection shown in moderation
but begin to lose my patience.

Is he giving her resuscitation?
No tongue separation in almost FOUR TUBE STATIONS!
And their performance doesn't end as we come to a stop,
a parade of people getting on while they're getting off.

PLEASE STAND CLEAR OF THE CLOSING JAWS

that open again as he explores her throat.
In incandescent drips of fluorescent light,
adolescents laugh and mothers avert children's eyes.
The gap they've created they don't seem to mind,

as they step off and head towards the London night.
Their lust escalating, as on the escalator they stand.
Smug smiles
linked limbs

and hand in hand.
Beaming, believing the world is their oyster card.
In future they should use taxis or tandems
or tinted windowed cars.

# Uneasy Jet

Today I'm a mess.
Riding alone on an Uneasy Jet.
Luggage checked.
Insides juggling inside out,
stirring up stress,
as I stir my coffee from the expensive food outlet.
No way out for my troubles – not even on the plane yet.
They trickle through my brain like the rain outside that the
puddles collect.
Select lunch from the eclectic food section in M&S,
something involving
'Mediterranean vegetables and watercress'.
Because an anxious passenger needs nothing less than the best.
There's no need to fret,
I'll be in Madrid by sunset.
Boarding passes with relative ease,
shared armrests and crushed up knees.
I push my head back in my plastic seat,
I breathe in deep,
as we leave the ground.
Through my tiny plane window, my last view of Bristol,
enveloped in grey clouds, all dripping with drizzle.
Back to my seat, attempt to stop being so neurotic,
headphones in, I lose myself in hypnotic harmonics.
And there's a forty something man across the aisle,
who wears a semblance of shame within his fixed on smile.
He gives me an
'oh my gosh! I was only reading this is in an ironic way!'
kind of look,
as he tries to carefully disguise his HARRY POTTER BOOK!

But he grabs my focus with his Hocus Pocus,
wrinkles his nose giving me a look of inherent mistrust,
as if he knows within my flows I'm verbally dexterous
and within my poetical prose I'll expose
his teenage boy-wizard love.
But up here there's no broomstick and no apparating,
this is what's known as standard aviation.
This is poetry in motion,
as I write down my emotion,
slightly baffled by the notion,
thirty thousand feet I'm floating
above a bottomless blue ocean.
But now I'm coming back down to Earth, quite literally,
thoughts floating, light-headed and dreamy.
Leave my seat and the faces I'll never see again,
clutching my baggage and a new perspective on reality.
Because when you're flying, you're defying gravity.
It does weird things to your mind,
makes you think philosophically
because what a strange thing it is in fact to even be,
just one thread in life's intricate tapestry.
So where better a place to question
how quickly life passes us by,
than in the aeroplane, bleaching white trails on
an endless canvas of sky.

# Shakespeare Was a Gangster Rapper

William Shakespeare was this nation's first ever great...
GANGSTER RAPPER.
A wordsmith warrior, a literary attacker
who literally created history,
a British Jay-Z for the 16th Century.
But for all of his wisdom, his wit and his flair,
every English teacher knows that pang of despair
when a child raises their hand and says
'Why do we have to learn this anyway?
It's not as if it relates to the youth of today'.
But Shakespeare does translate to the modern age.
Four hundred years on and all the world is still a stage,
Romeo's appertaining rage as Mercutio is slain
is the same as the gang violence that dominates the front page.
'To be or not to be' that is the question that still burns,
I'm not making Much Ado About Nothing,
just sit there and you'll learn
that he's talking about issues that we all struggle to handle,
like the swiftness of time 'out, out brief candle'.
And it's concepts like these that are constant you see
and capture the conscience universally.
Because like Hamlet 'never doubt I love'
and I'd rather 'bear the ills' of this world
than 'fly to others we know not of.'
We've all got those friends who we'd
'grapple unto our souls with hoops of steel'
and it is one man alone
who so eloquently sums up the way we all feel.
So that man you might have learnt about in English class,
well he's an unadulterated genius.

So to the poetical Prince of pentameter,
a cross generation communicator,
a trailblazing linguistic innovator,
an audience enthralling breath-bater,
an Elizabethan social commentator
who stills reigns supreme nearly half a millennium later.
He just sort of paved the way for Snoop Dogg and Kanye,
and he was as effective then as he is today.
So when it comes to expression there's nobody greater,
than the Bard
the poet
the gangster
William Shakespeare.

# 'Behind Every Great Christmas There's Mum'?

It's prime time for mulled wine and freezing in your britches,
and for celebrity Z-Listers, who make it their business,
to flick on town centre light show switches.
When we pretend that to an extent we're all vaguely religious,
while crooning to Cliff Richard
and having one too many glasses of Bucks Fizz with
home-baked star-shaped biscuits.
But just because it's Christmas,
does that really mean that I should be forced to witness,
companies so creatively listless
they feel need to depict us
as a nation whose population is in favour of such statements,
advocating the replacement of female vocation
with seasonal obligation to be sat alone over a stove slaving.
And I'm not just some mad 'feminist fundamentalist'
ranting and raving,
I'm just saying that
it seems crazy we're embracing
misogynistic depictions presented by ASDA-ian dictum,
whereby women must be prim, proper and Christian,
and only give birth to children
in order to spend Christmas in the kitchen.
Having no sense of own volition
under patriarchal systems
which are clearly non-existent.
While her family insist on
a swell of patronising applause
which only stands to reinforce
subservient slave is her dictionary definition.
And the slogan that we're given:
'Behind every great Christmas there's mum',

as if every female has or is one.
Attention to the male, they're giving none.
Because to ASDA being a dad doesn't matter,
it's just a matter of fact that
women are there to work hard and look perky,
to cook but not carve up the turkey,
and apparently I shouldn't let this 'irk' me,
but it hurts to see
this 21st Century ploy, that if you aren't born as a boy,
you're seen as devoid of any plausible function
under the assumption
that all you should live for is husband and mothering.
But I refuse to be smothered in
that stereotype of the narrow mind,
I'm inclined to find that real life acts as proof,
the agenda of gender that advertisers spew doesn't ring true.
Because men do as much as women do
and gender doesn't render
one sex more obligated to contribute.
It should be about Cointreau laced Christmas cake,
board games, too much food, bad TV and booze,
not profuse sexist platitudes based on antiquated views
so undue that they seek to undo
the equality we've fought to pursue.
So regardless of whether advertisements choose to listen
my sex will never be written by forced gender role divisions.
So this Christmas grab your glasses and lift them to
'Peace on Earth and good will to all men AND all women'
who refuse to be reduced to figments of supermarket
marketing fiction.

# Dadverts

I never had a Dad like the Dadverts,
incompetent and absent and averse
to cooking and cleaning, who watched football all evening
and never talked feelings.
I never had a Dad like the Dadverts.
I had the one who sang Joni Mitchell
two octaves higher than me,
held open the page folds of picture books
until one of us fell asleep,
who taught there's nothing I couldn't possibly achieve.
The kind inclined to cry at the films of Meryl Streep,
who believed equality,
never advocated misogyny
and raised his daughters properly,
to live long and prosper free.
And I remember, eight years old,
laughing because he listened to 'Woman's Hour',
as if it was funny that a man
gave worth to words of feminine power.
Because at that age the world is painted by numbers.
Primary colours:
Pink and Blue
and all seem invested in the truth
there's a difference between the two.
But I had the dad who drew horizons without boundaries,
forged my foundations like the fire from a foundry.
And I found he
was never the kind of dad to act blokey,
to drink eight pints in one night and say 'mate' colloquially,
but I had the one who opened me,
instilled hope in me.

He convinced me I could batter barriers with syllables,
that existence is a miracle,
to engage in things political.
And though sometimes things were difficult
I had a man whose influence is indivisible
from the sum of my being.
Encouraged dreaming,
was well-rounded and present,
a female voice advocate
and that's why I never had a Dad like the Dadverts.

# English Teacher

He fights the good fight every single day for not enough pay,
and an impending suspension of adequate pension,
which the Tory manifesto failed to mention.
True he may not save lives but he shapes and moulds minds.
And when kids choose to keep themselves blind,
there's not much to find behind the bravado
and the monosyllabic 'AND WHAT?'

To the beauty of the world and words they switch off,
their heads welded shut.
Every effort he makes is never enough, they don't give a ffff
'Fairer, faster, firmer!' Gove goads,
it's the teachers on which we need to be sterner.
As if the blatant lack of cooperation offered by the learner
doesn't affect the ability,
for a teacher to stand up and actually teach.

He's not asking them to appreciate the intricacy
in the work of Keats,
or believe in the worth of words that Wordsworth weaves.
Just to read.
A line
or two
or three.
To let him speak, without the need to shout over screams.
When babysitters become television screens,
these children lose their grasp on the depth of their dreams.
And so it seems that ignorance and attitude
are the things in life that come for free.
So they attack, snatch phone back from hard worked hands,
courtesy never factors into their punitive plans,

they'll do all that they can, without suspension or ban because
justice does not fight for the rights of an employed man.
Not just 'Mr Hill', he's Mr blood, sweat and tears,
every day he lives in fear
that the lessons he plans, no one will ever hear.
Because ears are shut off with headphones ,
but the kids that cause chaos never get sent home.
Now tell me Mr Gove,
should anyone have to carry that amount of baggage
as well as their marking home?
So how hard they work, you can continue to deny
but he's a superman by day and a father by night.
Longing not to have to fight
just to teach a single stanza or a verse.
Maybe it's people like him you should observe,
instead of slashing salary first,
if you could see how HARD they work,
relentlessly resilient.
You couldn't tell me he isn't worth a million.

# Lilah

You're the captain of the ship that I sail,
the fearless female
who never fails to amaze me.
Sincerity spills from the seams of every inch of your being.
You are ALL that you seem,
a constant stream of wild warmth and wit and dreams.
Your words batter artless patriarchal archetypal architecture
and casual misogyny.
Though you stand at less than 6 feet,
the height of your kindness overwhelms like mountain peaks.
You're a piece of me.
A carat gold slice of my soul, a joke that never gets old,
a never forget, 'je ne regrette', half of my whole.
And my whole being is singing, soul brimming with pride,
now I've heard that this brand new human being's
seeing the light of the world,
through the eyes of a baby girl for the first time.
And I hope that in my life, I will see you strive to defy
and redefine the female stereotype.
That you are wise,
shun pride
and blind others with a kind of kindness
born of mind over matter.
Because to me you'll always matter.
Like those scattered in corners and across borders of countries,
who anchor me and part the seas,
super-gluing their sentiments and sense
to the inner chamber where my heart beats.
And please always believe.
Breathe in dreams that are real not just for realms of sleep.

Smother your soul with ambitions and goals
and the pureness of poetry.
See the power profound found in endless amity.
If you're lucky you'll end up surrounded in the shelter
of fabulous feminine friends
who tie up all your lost loose ends,
befriend and mend you: just like me.
And I can see you're going to be utterly remarkable,
even right now at the very start of you.

# Stars

My soul sleeps on the cheek of a restless sky.
Silent night.
Whole universe sits solely to seduce my eyes
and infuse beauty into my being through sparkling jagged eyes
and ignite the hearts and minds in the world beneath.
And the life in my veins seems in vain,
gazing up at this dancing, endless, historical chain,
that has gazed upon centuries of human change,
and retained its strange ethereal beauty
in spite of all the terrible things that it's seen.
This canvas for mankind to paint its hopes upon,
to save souls and savour solace in the light they have shone.
On and on our fascination seems to grow,
with these sparkling fists
between whose wrists
sits everything that is known to exist
and where I find the words that fit and slip from these lips.
This is it.
These glass sparks that dance across the surface of the sky,
to remind us that even when we die,
there is light that will still shine,
inspiring minds like yours and mine.
And that's a comforting thought to rest my head upon tonight.

# Actor's church in the wake of Petrol/ Pastygate

'Foolery sir does walk about the orb like the sun,
it shines everywhere'
so even the air we breathe lies leaden with heavy dreams
that leaders have force fed us to believe
we can actually achieve to the point of obese.
But Cameron's abandoned his 'Big Society'
and Nick has 'Clegged' our aspiration arteries,
so this heart can't beat
or bypass the scars of your savage surgery,
imprison me with misery until I bleed tuition fees.
Because I have no appetite
for the kind of greed on which you feed,
but perhaps you can claw back some tax
if I quit fasting and live on Cornish pasties.
I'm hardly asking for you to part the seas,
but it startles me,
that these are streets
where children's nooses are tied by poverty lines
and lines of ink that make people think
are considered to be crimes.
Where NHS stands for 'No Hope Son'
and Olympics beats beating illiteracy
in the race for government funds.
And it's our fundamental flaw that we even ask for more than
your evasive,
pervasive party politics,
your spin storm.
But I warn you,
we'll fight your tempests relentless
throwing back the jerry cans you shove in our hands
until you understand

I believe everything you stand for is sickening.
So sit down, retire your reckless, restless rhetoric
and actually start listening.
Make some decisions.
Sort out the system.
Or better yet,
give me a Britain that's actually Great
and not this state that I live in.

# If Music Be the Food of Love

'If music be the food of love'
then why does discussing it always prove so tough?
Because I was brought up on Joni Mitchell and Fleetwood Mac,
while your parents raised you on The Jam  and The Clash.
And sometimes we do jam, but other times we clash,
like when you say
that Billy Bragg is music made exclusively for dads,
or Ben Folds Five are bad
or that new band I love are just a passing fad.
Because I don't have the time to know the latest trendy song,
and although I dislike them
I wouldn't come with you to bottle Mumford and Sons.
And yes sometimes I do sing Scissor Sisters in my kitchen
when nobody's listening
and ABBA and Beyoncé
when I'm trying to get the worktops glistening.
And I think that Kool and the Gang are actually quite cool,
and Wham and Madonna are great to dance to.
Even when we do agree
like when you state that 'Nick Drake is great'
there's still a point of debate
over which is better version one or two of Hazey Jane.
All the same, I think your taste is insanely good,
you show me bands I've never even heard of.
And sat in the back seat with the headphones,
on the way home,
we found a song that both of us hold close.
Carl Wilson's singing softly
but I feel like he's shouting out my soul
because what I'd be without you,well, 'God only knows'.

# Boyfriend on Holiday

Just thinking about when you'll arrive, mellows my mind
like the blissful corners of light that shine bright
through the side of sunglassed eyes.
But I don't take the time.
I pick a fight and lose sight and try to question WHY.
And that's not alright.
There's no excuse to tangle myself up in blue,
because I love this, I know you,
like back of hand,
track listings on the albums of all my favourite bands.
But I never planned to find a sand grain with my name on it,
so sometimes what I say is more ranting rage
than Shakespeare sonnet.
But honest,
I love those lazy laying around
with Lou Reed record Saturdays,
your imitation Jarvis Cocker dance moves
and eating cherry bakewells from the box for breakfast
on your birthday in a Glastonbury haze.
And his cakes are great but screw what Mr Kipling states
because we are the ones who are
'exceedingly good'.
Your heart creates sparks and warms mine like firewood.
In this jigsaw you fit adjacent, next to me
and if you fall out the box,
and become that piece doomed to be forever lost
beneath the settee never to be seen again,
you'll never puzzle me.
Because whether this endeavour is forever
or just now and then never,

I'll always be forced to admit,
that this brutal world is more beautiful with a 'you' in it.

# Vontrapped

When I was young I wanted to be a nun,
to run through a meadow
and bellow from the top of my lungs:
'the hills are alive with the sound of' fruitless
attempts to represent the endless eloquence of Julie Andrews,
the heaven sent soprano singer.
And I went too far, or so it seems,
I climbed every mountain in pursuit of my dreams.
It was my ultimate goal to solve a problem like Maria.
Couldn't stand to be Liesl or Brigitta,
it simply had to be her,
no matter how.
I couldn't kick the habit
having made one to wear out of a tea towel.
I'd howl and yodel the same old words,
like a lonely goatherd
in the high hills of Salzburg,
in an empty living room,
all afternoon,
believing every word was true.
So consumed I presumed that
brown paper packages tied up with string
had the potential to be one of my favourite things.
And that if you can sing it brings lightness to even the
gloomiest of occasions,
like escaping the incoming Nazi invasion.
This film was the persuasion
that an ex-naval officer makes the best kind of lover
and there was no man on Earth as dashing
as Christopher Plummer.
I wanted to have a Reverend Mother

and seven Austrian children whose singing talent I'd uncover.
But my plans were scuppered.
I was Vontrapped by the fact that
there wasn't a Nazi or nunnery in sight.
I didn't actually even believe in Jesus Christ.
And I was only seven years old,
couldn't sew and thus wouldn't know
how to use a needle pulling thread
to turn my curtains into clothes.
And I played that video so much it eventually broke
but as Maria said herself
'when God closes a door, he opens a window'.

# 99 Problems

I've got 99 Problems
and misogynistic vocabulary is one.
And even though I used to like that song,
I've got 99 Problems,
in a world where gender equality is too often forgotten,
and overbearing toxic doctrines of masculinity as sovereign
are increasingly common.
Nothing can soften the sadness of sitting watching,
TV screens spouting seedy scenes of half-dressed teens
uncovered for covers of magazines.
And one day my tutor told me
that she had sat with other mothers struggling
summoning names of women in public eye,
who offered ample positive example.
Reformers, reinforcers of the possibilities their daughters
could have within their lives.
And that made me want to cry.
To think I live in a world,
where little girls are only shown role-models
that teach a woman's role is model, or mother,
footballer's wife or lover, insignificant other.
It's not enough to
say that Maggie and May make it all ok
that less than twenty five percent
of MPs that represent the UK today are women.
And maybe one day newspapers will make the decision,
to cut the front pages
dedicated to dissecting feminine physique,
and instead choose to speak about rape victims
being stoned to death in Iran.
Give over the column inches devoted

to the 'unconvincing size' of 'our Kate' and her baby bump
to Caitlin Moran,
to people who actually give a damn
about equality prevailing between woman and man.
With all that I am I implore
give me more Mary Beards,
more Germaine and Bonnie Greers,
women known for their careers,
and respected by their peers, for the wisdom of their years.
And if I ever choose to have a child
I will never let them live in fear.
Because be it a daughter or a son
they will have a million and ninety-nine options
and a 'bitch' will not be one.

# Glastonbury

Glastonbury is tangled traffic jams, perpetual precipitation
and rowdy music fans.
'Puerile playground', 'ideological wasteland',
free of logical people
just free love and free loaders.
Where peace gets preached by matted hair hippy priests
and everything becomes a commentary,
narrated upon incessantly by a smiling Jo Whiley.
Perhaps that's what you think if you've only seen it on the BBC
but that's not what this place means to me.
Glastonbury is an exoteric exodus,
a sense of amity
as you amble amongst the anonymous and amorous.
It takes the mundane, turns it archaic and arcane,
where your local shop is a man selling batteries and loo roll
while wearing a top hat!
What tops that?
Peer behind the frenetic aesthetic and find a prophetic setting
in which to count your blessings.
Where time lies in our hands
and not the ones on our wristwatch
and bankers wear wellies
and attempt to 'find themselves' by getting lost,
and they sing 'I want to live like common people', is that ironic
or what?
Because they represent everything this festival is not.
It's not about earning a badge about which you can brag,
it's Billy Bragg, spirits that never sag,
smiles that last and the long day drag of muddy feet.
It's the man that goes manic while holding a microphone,
the sense of feeling that you're never alone,

it's ripping off your skin and dancing around in your bones.
It's the sunset still emblazoned on my retinas,
the stage to stage dash, endless pursuit of the thrill,
It's flamingos on stilts
and learning to be hazy and lazy and chilled.
It's joy that's undistilled, being all that you can.
It's your boyfriend's mum going to watch Ray Davies
and coming back a raving Faithless fan.
It's a cup of chai and a slice of life shared with strangers
who rebuild the temple of your mind.
It's the poet's tongue that bleeds out beauty,
his sole goal to expose his soul for the rest of us to see.
It's the clutch of your nose as you head to the long drop.
Silk flags that whisper in the wind
and become the rooftops.
It's that moment.
Head back, hand in air,
headlong sing-along shared with 100,000 others.
It's the simplest of truths only now you've uncovered.
Found in sky lanterns, falafel and the smell of firewood,
that life is precious and vital and vibrant and good.
It's grass at your elbows
and love that spills out from the seams.
Now that is what I call Glastonbury.

I know this reads like a woefully self-indulgent Oscars acceptance speech but I would like to thank...

**All the Bluestocking girls**, past and present. **Mary Beard**, a fabulous female, a 'classy, classic classicist', for kindly supporting this book and for being what I want to be when I grow up! **Burning Eye Books** for making a book with my name on the front cover. **Rachel**, for being the kind of English teacher who writes the lives of her students. For encouraging me to put a pen in my hand in the first place and for innumerable reassurances once it was there. **Joelle Taylor**, for taking me from impromptu poem shouting on Covent Garden pavements to the Royal Festival Hall. **Ally**, for being the best cheerleader a young poet could wish for during your time at the Poetry Society, always being on hand with Revels and shivery conversations at the bus stop. **All the rest at the Poetry Society** for continued kindness in supporting my career. **My fellow SLAMbassadors**, inspirationally talented in every way. **Nils**, for enduring countless performances and three and a half years. **Charlie and Jessie**, for being my foremost and formative friends. **Aggie and Bonnie**, the best malenky droogs a devotchka could ask for. My flatmate **Kate**, for editing my anxiety out of these poems, allowing me to act out the Sound of Music to her at 1am and still wanting to live with me! **Aja**, you remarkable, wild, brilliant being, I could not do this life thing without you! **Imogen Ruby Free**, 'a bosom friend – an intimate friend, you know – a really kindred spirit to whom I can confide my inmost soul.' You have no idea! **Kimmy**, for your many Northern charms – God is your garden in Blundell Sands. **The English Department at King's College London**, for being a great supportive force behind this book and for the incredible work you all do. Your lectures make me happy! Particularly for the **female academics**, who I am incomparably inspired by and aspire to be on a daily basis. **Adelene** for being unflinchingly kind when 'it was the worst of times', non-contractually obliged conversations on Dickens and Mark Owen in equal measure and reminding me 'the glass may be empty but at least now there is a tap!' This book would not have been written without your support. **Laura Bates** and the Everyday Sexism Project, for being lovely and offering hope to us all! **My two shining sisters** who I admire and envy in equal measure. **Dad**, for never being like the 'Dadverts'. **Mum**, for always knowing what to do! **The family and friends** who tie up all my loose ends. And, most importantly, **to all the kind ears from across the years and the lovely people attached to them**, this is for you...

Lightning Source UK Ltd.
Milton Keynes UK
UKOW05f0435311216
291127UK00004B/43/P